The Art of finishing stuff that matters

A hands-on guide about productivity, activation energy,

motivation and procrastination – not only for entrepreneurs.

How to eat a mammoth?

Bite after bite

Unknown

TABLE OF CONTENT

1   Foreword

Have you ever asked for a 10% discount at Starbucks? That would need a lot of courage and energy, no? But are you back up right after and dispelled the cellar for years waiting for you? Who does not know these seemingly mammoth tasks that are repeatedly postponed and planned and scheduled thereafter. These larger (and smaller) things that we actually have long wanted to do. If we had to hunt every morning the first thing for a mammoth, so that our family has something to eat, would we not do it? Or are we going to wait until the mammoth comes to us from the cave and politely requests to be eaten? You may want to say: we live in the year 2016 and mammoth no longer exists - but I'm sure you know what I mean.

In the last 20 years, I repeatedly searched for advice, coaching, productivity apps, methods and tricks of all kinds, but nothing really seemed to work. It was like a virtuous circle; I noticed the real key to real productivity lies within us; we feel it, we know it, and of course, we know when we should do it. Being unproductive hurts us more than it feeds our laziness and every so often we ask ourselves over and over again what we are going to do to fix it. I totally understand because I've been there.

I am an entrepreneur myself and I belong to the famous Generation Y. We can and may do anything - not because we are very good at it, but simply because it is possible. We do not make it right all the time, but we have all the options. However, we all get those days when we can't seem to get anything done, better or worse; we try to make things work all to no avail. Sound familiar? Then this book is for you. In this book, I reveal several ideas and methods that I have been using in the last 20 years, have been living through and through. I will provide you with a hands-on tour how you can manage to get more out of your time.

Note that, this is not some bunch of tools and tricks from the varied options you already have out there. No. Neither is it another "How to become more productive" guide. It's about things that you probably already heard, forgotten or have thought impossible, such as the chemistry behind the activation energy which builds the 80/20 rule of time management or the 90/10 rule the planning, the consistent application for the efficient completion of tasks, and this flow state, of which we have all probably heard or even been.

Neither is this a miracle or wizard spell of some kind: lets face it, its work, hard work even and we must get into it, step by step – or bite by bite. We will get to the mammoth eventually and hunt it down – by the time you will realize: it's just a hairy elephant.

2   The reasons for reading this book

There are days when we all wonder how we have spent our time. We begin to blame ourselves for wasting the entire day, considering the unnecessary details when we ought to focus on the most important things. At the end of the day, we feel we haven't done anything at all. Most of the time, the cause would be because we have procrastinated to do the major things, and only focus on the less stressful and less important things.

I have not been a great procrastinator from my school days but I always had trouble finishing stuff. But over the years, I have defined a strategy of procrastination that works for me at last but not entirely, which is why this book was written. I discovered that when you do not finish a particular task, the mental stress alone is enough to make you feel worthless. You know that feeling of 'I know I should have done it' or 'I will definitely do it later'? Before you know it, the time gets really close and you see that the mental stress increases, too.

For me, it got so bad I would spend the entire day reading emails, drinking coffee, chatting on social media, texting random contacts, and before you know it, it's evening already, and I'd be like 'what the heck have I done today?' I'd then encourage myself to do it first thing tomorrow morning only to repeat the same pattern through the next day.

If you can relate to this, then make sure you read this book from cover to cover, from start to finish and again and again. Because in here in lies the exact blueprint you need to overcome that lifestyle forever. If any page strikes you, you are free to circle, markup or highlight it, so you can come back to it at a later stage. This book is your guide and counselor, you may use it to create your own hands-on guide. Or if you get into this state of "I should do but how do I do it", so anytime you get stuck, you can always come back to this book for practical tips and inspiration for your next step. These tips are easy to implement, and the best part is, I am willing to show you everything.

Now, let's get started, shall we?

"If we did all the things to which we are capable of,

we would surprise ourselves."

Thomas A. Edison

3   My story and how I got to the topic

As a child, I was curious and diligent, but that wasn't enough for me to get good grades. I was always distracted, not well organized, had other priorities, or so it seemed. I tried all I could but nothing seemed to work. Even when I wanted to become an electrical engineer, I tried to get all the studies and assignments done, the trainings to be sharp and highly productive, but unfortunately I always found something more exciting and then failed at engineering. 20 years later, I started the adventure of being an entrepreneur, but this also came to a dead end in the first run. I constantly asked myself: Why? I wanted to find out and began to read – a lot actually, maybe like you. A few dozen talks, 60 Guides, 800 hours of YouTube videos and tens of thousands of internet articles later it downed on me: there was no help out there. Ant the worst: there was no tool or technology that could change my situation and help me becoming more successful and more productive – I simply wasn't. But I didn't want to accept this either. I wanted to understand what really drove this. The problem was much deeper buried.

Remember back in the days, during school, we were told we could do anything and everything, if we want to? Oh you are performing poor in Mathematics? Learn more and you will succeed. No success in sports so far? Increase the training. But something's seemed not quite right? Why were the mathematicians not good at sports and some of the sporty guys and girls had problems in history or languages? We weren't those "Jack of all trades", were we? We do have a talent that's for sure. We obtain interests and abilities, in which we are a little better than others. But there is a catch: There is one thing that we are really, really good at: talent. We just need to find out a) what it is and b) what keeps us from getting them mastered.

4   Activity is not the same as performance

We can all work at any time and perform anywhere: communicate, shop, write, play, and even sleep. Time and resources are unlimited available in a steady online and connected world - regardless of the falsely suggestion that we are multitasking jack-of-all-trades and universal talents. Because at the same time, we do less and less and leaving a lot of things unfinished. Maybe we are not really good at what we do, and that itself overwhelms us constantly and we start new things just to prove we are wrong. We actually do know what we have to do or what we have to say no to - like too many distractions - and there are certain tasks that are better, more lucrative and more fun than others put together. We would know that if we were more honest with ourselves and had some system to bring it into. We just need to find out which of these tasks are more fitting for us – but how do we find that out?

Constantly talking, making plans and writing concepts without doing something are all useless, if we do not really implement and make things happen. But we can change that fact. The first step: block your calendar on a daily routine. Every day set aside 30 or 60 minutes for the most important tasks. Block it. Maybe after lunch, or just when you got home. Or you can't do it because you have a demanding job? Get up earlier – just 30 minutes, that won't hurt, would it? Because if you succeed in that matter. This would mean by that at the end of the year – counting for 300 days as there are some holidays and very important events as well - you have invested about 150 hours into the things that matter most and towards the realization of our goals. That's huge! 150 hours or 20 work days at 8 hours! What can you all accomplish within almost a month? Every piece you can set aside counts, because it adds up. This is called the compound effect; those incremental improvements, small steps that lead us to huge goals at the end of the day.

But we need to *activate, discipline* and *persevere* ourselves – or short: *ADA* - only when you become a goal and action-oriented person who which is active, reliability and performance-driven can you achieve your goals or make more of your talent.

Also important: You must take a step further every day: walk 20 minutes to learn 10 new words, do 5 pushups, and meditate for 5 minutes. Bring yourself to make. Do some sets of something that brings you those kinds of endorphins – mostly those are things that bring us happiness. What if you know exactly what you ought to do but cannot get started? Then what you may need is your Motivation and activation energy (See for that Chapter 11).

But be careful, do not waste your time on little or less significant things, no matter how enticing they sound or how quick a motivation it promises just because they can be done quickly.

Remember you have only 1440 minutes every day, and a power battery of 100% decreases in energy as the clock ticks, so it's up to you to devote the right time to your most important tasks early enough before your energy level drops. You don't believe me? Well let's dive into it further.

"Look at a day when you are supremely satisfied at the end.

It's not a day when you lounge around doing nothing;

it's a day you've had everything to do and you've done it."

Margaret Thatcher

5   The difficulty about difficult things

If you were to do one thing first in the morning, what would it be, and which is the most difficult for you? Chances are, you will become more successful and more relaxed doing exactly that ONE thing. Do you believe me? Have you tried? Is there something that's really on your mind for very long? Then do it – come on, start now and then come back reading. If you have done that, you will feel great and then we can begin our journey.

Because the problem is simple: time flies faster, mountains of e-mails, whatsapp, Messengers, social media, and despite all the digital assistants in the world, we still have less time for the really important things. The ridiculous thing about it is that, we all have the same amount of time; from the politicians to the midwife, from student to retiree, we all equally have 1440 minutes.

Nevertheless, we are not effective enough. Warning, it is not about efficiency: We do not want more stuff in our everyday lives, what we want is to concentrate on the really important and essential ones. True to the Pareto principle (80:20 rule), we want to know what things provide us 80% of the results in 20% of the time. We can then focus on those things that give us the best results and double or triple our productivity as the case may be.

Why most time problems cannot be solved easily is because we think we need more of it to be able to do more meanwhile, what we actually need is to focus on the 20% that gives us the 80% results we seek. That is, we do not change the tool but our attitude.

Just like the saying, 'if you have both hands full, you can't hold anything more until you let go', so it is with time. And that's why you have done this one thing that was on your mind for so long now – and if you haven't despite my advice: just do it now.

"The most efficient way to live reasonably is to make a plan of one's day every morning and every night examining the results obtained."

Alexis Carrel

6   Getting the Flow

Do you remember how you have felt after that one big thing you have accomplished. Or while being at an exam and you were in the topic? Or that one book, that one movie that sucked you in unlike anything else before? Then maybe you have heard of that perfect wave. I do not refer to the wave in terms of surfing, but that state in which one is completely absorbed in his task. For instance, the video game that your daughter wants to play and won't do anything until she finishes, the sporting event that you do not want to miss and then forget about the food in the oven? Or the moment you are engrossed in your favorite reading, riddle or tutorial that you do not hear when we try speaking with you? If yes, then you have been in the flow. The most important step to being productive therefore is to direct this to what you do. But how do you get into this state, especially if we are talking about some pounding or highly concentrated tasks?

The truth is, it not always as easy to be in the flow with real tasks like you'd be with games or books, but that doesn't mean it is not possible. It is the state of peak performance; a place where you operate at your best, where the seemingly hard stuff flows naturally and it amazes you how you could pull that off. In short, it is the state we always would love to be.

The question now is how do you get in the flow state?

The world's greatest thinkers have described the flow state as the most productive and creative state of mind in which to work. In addition, positive psychologists–most notably Dr. Mihaly Csikszentmihalyi, Ph.D. – argue that achieving the flow state on a regular basis is a key component of happiness. That is, by learning how to enter the state of flow you can increase your productivity, be more creative, and be happier, all at the same time.

Here's how a leading composer described the flow state, *"You are in an ecstatic state to such a point that you feel as though you almost don't exist. I have experienced this time and again. My hand seems devoid of myself, and I have nothing to do with what is happening. I just sit there watching it in a state of awe and wonderment. And [the music] just flows out of itself."* Interesting, isn't it? You see, if you must succeed as an entrepreneur, you must be able to 'get in the flow' every so often, especially when it comes to tasks that require your full attention. The truth is, many tasks actually would require all your attention when you are running a real business, which makes this expedient. The following points will help:

1. **Find Something Your Love Doing** – Pick up something that you enjoy doing; it could be playing with piano, skiing, golfing, etc. Chances are you are likely to hit the flow state faster when you do something you love.

2. **Work On Your Skills** – The more competent you are regarding a thing, the easier it would be to enter into the flow state. You struggle more with something you find difficult to do. But when you have mastered a skill, it becomes much easier.

3. **Set vivid goals** – The more sure you are about what you want to do, the less divided your attention, and when your attention is totally on to something, you are closer to the flow state that ever.

4. **Work only on the task at hand** – Nothing else, just the task at hand. Jumping from one task to the other only creates confusion and lack of focus.

5. **Set enough time for each task** – Yes, when you set little time for what would normally take more time, you get mentally constrained to let your creative juices flowing because the anxiety of having limited time keeps you from getting into the flow state.

Now get a piece of paper. Write your most important task of today on it. Below write three (just three) things you want to have completed by today. Do you get the picture? Look at it and think how you would feel once you have finished it all. But wait do not start yet. You need more.

One secret ingredient: Maybe you found all those playlists on YouTube or Spotify that have some Beats per Minute (BPM) of over 140. If you are not so much into that mostly drum and base stuff or hard-rock, pick a playlist of great, motivational songs with lots of drums, you must feel that rhythm inside you. Listen to it and wait, wait until you cant wait no more and then start walking. Just walk and follow the music. You might even start running. If you like that feeling, keep that in mind and save that playlist for the next time you wan to get into this state of flow.

The freedom to do your best means nothing unless you are willing to do your best

Colin Powell

7 ADP - activation, discipline, perseverance

A Chinese proverb says: "Even the longest journey begins with a single step". Complex tasks deter and often the beginning is repeated delays. It helps to share such a project into small subtasks and then just start – with the methods described before. The most important task, the three things, that underlying music beat.

However, you must understand the end goal and have that picture in mind. Then break it down but backwards. What are the steps to get there but in reverse order? How many steps are there? Three, five or even ten? Once you know that list of subtasks it is very important to start with those baby steps and work through them gradually until you reach your goals. This will not only make the work faster, but also easier because you are working on it in smaller batches as opposed to juggling between a bunches of tasks. It is comparable to the law of inertia or Newton's first law of motion that states, an object will continue to be in motion in a straight line unless an external force acts on it.

Overall, it is very important to stay organized, having a clear picture of the end goal, and then splitting the tasks to make it easier to achieve that end goal. Change this sequence only when it cannot be avoided (for example, because the original order of a logic error involves) and not because of a personal preference. This is where the ADP principle works best; start the tasks in bits (activation), be resolute about getting it done (discipline), and the follow through until you hit the target (perseverance). Now, let's look at each one individually:

Activation

Activation simply means to set in motion what is static. It can also be seen as starting an activity with the goal of achieving a specific target. This also applies to tasks or our individual entrepreneurial activities and processes. During activation, you picture the processes involved in getting the project done, draw out a reasonable plan of action, and then set in motion that process. This is the first step to doing anything worthwhile.

Discipline

Now that you have put in motion the task at hand and have cut down the tasks into reasonable chunks, you have to commit yourself into following the activation plan by starting with the first subtask. This is where your loyalty or passion for the project is tested. It shows how committed or willing you are with achieving the end result. The truth is, if you must actually get the job done; this is a key step because nothing worthwhile can be achieved without discipline. You cannot do the tasks at your own convenience; you have to follow through asset plan. And that leads us to the next step.

Perseverance

Someone defined perseverance as stick-to-it-effectiveness. It means sticking to a particular task, no matter how difficult it looks, until successful. Truth is we will (and have) come across tasks that almost always want us to throw in the towel, but success demands perseverance. Your strength of character will always be tested with each task, and it proves how touch an entrepreneur you are; one that easily gives in to defeat or one with the mind of a champion, which won't take no for an answer until they achieve the needed result.

"It is not that we have so little time but that we lose so much. ... The life we receive is not short but we make it so; we are not ill provided but use what we have wastefully."

Lucius Annaeus Seneca

9   The importance of activation energy

You must understand that it is absolutely essential that we are not always effective and motivated. Our energy balance is a fragile and multi-stage and multi-tier system. We need food, water, light, calm, stimulation and emotions and the different in very subjective masses. We are humans.

And we humans take the path of least resistance. So we must ensure that this path leads up to the positive results or the good habits. We have to blaze this trail for ourselves accordingly. Many proposals to change habits or to overcome procrastination follow this pattern. So what can we do? The idea is always the same: reduce the energy needed to start the task, or keep the level of resistance it as low as possible. Because here comes our daily paradox: As long as the task at hand takes more activation energy required as it causes stress, there is a risk for slipping. We call this little input of "starting" something "activation energy".

This activation energy, coined in 1889 by Svante Arrhenius, is an energy barrier that must be overcome in a chemical reaction of the reactants. In general the lower the activation energy existing, the faster the reaction.

So you can just follow this physic principle. Decrease the activation energy needed for tasks that you want to do. For example: what about the habit to plan the work of the next day the night before. Or that the first job for the next morning already is set on the desk the evening before. Or you can put your running shoes next to the bed, if you want to start running the same morning. Or if I should finally fill an office tax form, instead of doing so, I could pin it to the wall just to anticipate the small step and to lower the hurdle of starting something.

And on the other hand of course: lift the energy hurdle up at things that distract you from doing the essentials. If your deferral strategy is to quickly check the news, social media or to check the latest status of a share price, simply delete the bookmark in the browser, so that you have to enter the URL manually. You may also decide not to save the password and to force myself to type it every time. Or I use a special browser plugin, which saves me from entering such sites; it's just a small 20-second hurdle of installing this piece of software. The software can be found under the term "distraction-free" software and is based on the principle, of simply blocking certain applications on the computer in order to build barriers against the bad habits.

So what can you do? Decrease the hurdles of starting and increase the hurdles in terms of energy when it comes to distraction potentials. Do it now, and today, you may start with this software here. It's important to note, however, that these types of software/tools are not a solution, but tools to aid your new habits of focus and time management. It's best to learn new habits of simplifying, clearing distractions, staying mindful of the task you're working on. These tools can help you get started, but they're not absolutely necessary, and if you do use them at first you might find you don't need them forever.

Mac Freedom

An extreme tool but an effective one. Disables your entire Internet connection for a time period set by you. Perfect when you really need to focus for an hour or three at a time.

Selfcontrol

Disable access to mail servers and websites that distract you. For example, you could block access to Facebook, Gmail, Twitter, and your favorite blogs for 90 minutes, but still have access to the rest of the web. Once started, you can't undo it until the timer runs out.

Concentrate

Create an activity (design, study, write, etc.) and choose actions (launch or block websites, quit applications, speak a message, and more) to run every time you concentrate. When ready, just click "concentrate." All your distractions will disappear and a timer will appear to help you stay focused.

„The first requisite for success is the ability to apply your physical and mental energies to one problem incessantly without growing weary."

Thomas A. Edison

10   Clarity and discipline = Productivity

Do you know what you want exactly? Perhaps you do have a goal, or you don't have a goal. When speaking of "goals" this term will include any number of specific tasks, which need to be completed, from household chores to major business proposals. Tasks to be performed are referred to as either short, medium, or long-term goals, depending on the available time the individual has to complete them. Short-term goals may be thought of as daily goals. These often include everyday chores, as well as projects, which need to be completed immediately. In effective time management a list of short terms goals is formulated, and each goal on that list is completed, on a daily basis.

Let me make an example: as children we were always clear about what we wanted; it could be to get a gift or to spend the weekend away with friends. In order to achieve that we were told what we needed to do.

8 steps for greater effectiveness

You can double your effectiveness or triple if you know why and how you do it. This requires a no project plan. For more productivity you need clarity. Why clarity you may say? You need to know what is needed and why! Why do you do that task? What is it for? What's your motivation behind it? Do write this down and it sets energy and emotions freely. An

American saying goes: Emotion Creates Motion - emotion generates movement. And this can also mean: Once started (motion) it brings positive feelings (emotions) that keeps you going.

You may proceed as follows:

1. Set a goal and say to yourself: why
2. You think with paper: write objectives make them valuable
3. Get an urgent deadline - you need to stress
4. Make a list of steps that you must do, to finish
5. Arrange the list in order of priority and dependence
6. Begin immediately. And it is only the first step on the list. You must be active.
7. Plan 'a one step to join every day 5, 10 or 20 more.
8. Invest 10% in the proper planning and 90% in the reaction. You must know and understand what to do.

"Starting is strength,

finishing is true power."

Laotse

11   Persistent until its finished

Every so often we get certain impulses, better said, some creative curiosity to try new things, engage in a new challenge and somehow we get used to it. Many other times however, we lose the initial enthusiasm and give up on what was once like a burning desire. We ask ourselves why, but the answer never comes. There are many factors that could be responsible for such, but the most delicate one is the lack of focus and persistence.

The entrepreneurial journey is never for the feeble-minded; to succeed as an entrepreneur and build a business that can stand the test of time, you need to be focused and persistent. It is like the lifeblood of running any business. Lack of focus could cost you way more than the business itself; your reputation will also be as stake. So now, let's discuss how to stay focused.

How can we stay focused?

Focus takes training. It is not something that comes overnight neither is it an innate ability some people was born with; you have to train your brain for it. Obviously as an entrepreneur, you have so much on your plate that is simultaneously calling your attention. The lack of focus would mean choosing the wrong thing over the other and ruining the entire process. The following tips should help:

1. **Ensure you take on the most difficult task first** – Naturally, we tend to do the less difficult task first. You know, we like ease and the feeling of accomplishing those little tasks seem to boost our confidence to take on the more difficult ones. To stay focused however, you have to face the most difficult first because "every decision we make tires the brain" and making the decision to take on the easier alternative would have the same effect as taking on the more difficult one.

2. **Set the right time deliberately** – research has it that we are truly focused for an average of only six hours per week, so it is expedient you try and be more deliberate in what you put into those hours. While the time differs for most people, you have to figure when your best focus time is. When is it that you often experience that aha moment? If you know this, you will be more focused.

3. **Train your mind to stay focused** – the mind is a powerful tool and for you to master being focused, you have to train it like a muscle. We are in an era where distractions are everywhere. The good thing however is that we can at least try to reduce these

distractions to the barest minimum. It may not be easy, but we have to try to constantly train our minds to stay focused. Practice concentration by turning off all distractions and committing your full attention to a single task.

Now that we have considered how to stay focused, we would look at how to stay persistent.

How can we stay persistent?

Just like being focused, being persistent is a skill you can develop. Like we mention in previous chapters, being persistent requires that you:

1. Break down your tasks into bit sizes. This will reduce the anxiety involved in taking on big projects.
2. Reward yourself after each success. Celebrating little successes help you stay persistent, as you will always be looking forward to subsequent rewards.
3. Do something you enjoy doing. When your task is what you love to do, it becomes a natural part of the process. It becomes a passion and something you never want to stop doing.

Staying persistent is something every entrepreneur should learn. Make it a priority to train your brain constantly to stay focused because it is only through that you will achieve great success.

"You have to allow a certain amount of time in which you are doing nothing in order to have things occur to you, to let your mind think.

Jerome Mortimer Adler

12   Motivation impulses

Imagine if you were to focus on a single task at a go. Imagine waking up and going to the gym as though working out is all you have to do. Your mind is blank besides the fact that you want to work out or exercise. Guess what would happen; you will do it with the best of your abilities. You will then have breakfast, enjoying every aroma and flavor of the fresh sumptuous meal. You pick up a book to read and you focus on it as if nothing else matters. You then head over to work, focusing on one task at a time, with all your phones and notifications silent as though that is all you have to do. Just imagine how that feels. The following motivation impulses will help.

Live in the moment

Nothing beats a life lived fully in the moment; it gives you the privilege of enjoying every minute of it. It helps you better appreciate what you do and encourages you to put in everything you've got to bring the best out of it, no matter what the task is about. Needless to say, you will become more focused, work more effectively, become much better at what you do, appreciate time more, enjoy the beauty of nature through the things around you, and live a distraction-free life.

Develop being conscious

Learn to become more aware of whatever it is you are doing when starting it. Start it as though it is the only thing you have to do, really focus on it and clear off every distraction around you. Determine to stay on this one thing only. This is the first step.

Clear all distractions

If you're working on a PowerPoint presentation, clear everything else away, so you have nothing but you and your computer. If you're going to reply or send emails, close every other program and all browser tabs except the email tab, and just do that. If you're going to do a work task, have nothing else open, and turn off the phone or silent all notifications. If you're going to eat, put away the computer and other devices and shut off the television. This might not be easy initially, but constant practice will train your mind to quickly adapt.

Choose your tasks wisely

After you have carefully written down your To Do list, before you start doing a task, give it some thought — do you really want to call that client right now? you really want to do email right now? Is this the most important work task can be doing at the moment? Sometimes timing matters a lot; it determines level of enthusiasm we put into a particular task. Carefully selecting what you have to do per time helps you better focus and put your all into it.

Really pour yourself into it

If you're going to send that email, do it with complete focus and dedication. Do not reply an instant message, a whatsapp or similar while doing your email. Put everything you have into that activity. If you're going to have a conversation, really listen and really be present. If you're going to make your bed, do it with complete attention and to the best of your abilities.

Pick just a few tasks each day

Yes. You may have been told to keep a long list of everything you are to do each day, but the truth is, keeping such a bogus list can kill your enthusiasm and make it look overwhelming even before you start working on them. Instead, make a short list — just 1-3 things you really want to accomplish. Call this your 'MUST DO' list. As explained in the first chapter, these should be extremely important tasks that will have a high-impact on your business.

Make sure your do your MUST DO tasks first

Focus on these most important tasks first and do nothing else until you have completed them. Refuse to check your emails, Facebook, Twitter, blogs, online forums, news sites, etc. Start your day after making your short list by working on your first MUST DO task.

Learn to stop yourself if you want to falter

This happens sometimes, especially when you are starting out. While working on your MUST DO tasks, you may feel that urge to check your email, or switch to something more interesting in a bid to run away from stress – stop yourself. Breathe deeply. Re-focus yourself. Get back to the task at hand. If other things come up while working on any particular task, note them on a piece of paper small notebook. These are notes for things to do or follow-up on later, or ideas. Just take a short note, and then get back to the task at hand. This way you do get sidetracked, but you also don't forget those things you need to remember later.

Occasionally relax

Take deep breaths, stretch, and take breaks now and then. Enjoy life. Go outside, and appreciate nature. Keep yourself sane.

Practice

Just like mastering anything else, this type of distraction-free life is not something you'll learn to do overnight. You can start right now, but you're likely to be good at it at first. Keep at it. Practice daily, throughout the day. nothing else, but practice until you become really good at it.

"People love chopping wood.

In this activity one immediately sees results."

Albert Einstein

13   Planning makes productivity visible

Yes you read that right: planning. For productivity to happen, you need to have a solid plan, something that becomes a burning passion, and something that guides you into effective actionable steps towards achieving your goals. It's like telling your mind what you have on your plate and how you want to accomplish it. Abraham Lincoln once said: If I had to cut down a tree in 5 hours, I would use four hours sharpening my ax and then cut down the tree in an hour. Think about that carefully.

Remember that 10 minutes each day saves you 120 minutes of time and energy in 12 days. Thinking this way helps you better plan your time and get something tangible done. Now, the question is, how do you plan effectively?

How to plan effectively

Planning is a critical step towards achieving anything worthwhile in life. But many people do not know how to plan their time effectively.

These points will help you:

1. **Focus on the end result and try to visualize it** – seeing the end before you even start is one of the best steps towards effective planning. I say that because, when you can visualize where you are

headed, you are half way there. You know exactly what to put in place to get there.

2. **Embrace some solitude** – yes, get into a quiet plan where you can think without interruption. This will help your mind focus on the end result you have seen and then be able to come up with something clear and precise about the process.

3. **Ask yourself very critical questions** – planning entails some thorough analysis of what can and what cannot work. Asking yourself certain kinds of questions gets you prepared for the unimaginable. A solid plan required some solid bases by which decisions are made. You can't have those bases when you have not personally asked yourself certain questions. Questions like, how feasible is this project? What is the target audience? How can you effectively market the products to reach the target audience? Etc.

Now that you know how to plan effectively, you may want keep something in mind; always focus on the end goal. Be clear about where you are headed. Without this clarity, it will be difficult to set the right plans in motion towards achieving it.

How to proceed? Take out a piece of paper and pen and start writing down your plans, keeping in mind what we have discussed above.

"You cannot manage your time,

you can only manage your focus."

Michael Kastner

14   What lists you must manage

We all make a list every so often about what we want to do. It could be a to-do list of our daily activities, weekly or even monthly plan. Be it a list containing our short term or long term plans, you need to be able to manage them effectively. The thing, most times, we end up never following the list we have carefully written, because, of course, things change. Plans get expanded and then we lose focus and trash the remaining items on the list. If that resonates with you, you are not alone. We've all been there, but how do we take care of these lists to ensure we follow through till we accomplish every single item on it? We will consider how for each of the lists below.

Master List

Master list is the grand plan vividly put on paper about a particular project or our lives. It contains everything you want to do. A master plan could contain all the steps needed to make a certain project a success. This list is usually extensive and covers every area of the project. However, because of its extensiveness, we often become overwhelmed from having so much to do on our master list. It could contain up to 50 items that ought to be done. To manage this master plan, make sure you are as clear as possible with the items on the list. Be realistic and confident that what you have on the list is actually doable. This will go a long way to helping you better plan the monthly, weekly or daily steps that would aid you to accomplish what you have on the master list. When writing your master list, make sure you don't include any urgency as that will cause unnecessary anxiety that might stall the entire process. It's okay to set a timeline for the big picture, but make sure you are realistic about that. Also note that, how vivid the master list is, determines how the other lists would follow.

Monthly list

A monthly list is a list of items that you want to accomplish within 30 days or 31 days, as the case may be. This list is often derived from the master list as it reflects a few of the steps in the master list. Depending on the duration of the goals on the master list, the monthly list doesn't have to contain everything on the master list. Choking yourself with so much only complicate things for you and help you stay rather unproductive. A monthly list is a list of carefully selected items from your master list with the goal of taking one step at a time. Also note, do not take more than you can chew; pick the items based on priority to be done within the month (30 or 31 days).

Weekly list

Your weekly list should contain realistic goals for the week from what you already have on your monthly list. Remember you have 7 days in a week, so make sure you set realist goals that are achievable so you don't overwhelm yourself and end up not doing anything at all. It is better to do small things well than overwhelm yourself with so much that you can't do anything. As the age old saying, little is much when it comes to effectiveness. Never forget that.

Daily list

This is what we are already used to as entrepreneurs. Every morning we wake up and the first thing we do is writing down what we need to do for the day. The mistake most people make with their daily lists is that, it is not tied to a master, monthly or weekly list. When you are found of waking up and coming up with fresh ideas or goals to pursue, you can barely achieve much as an entrepreneur. Let your daily goals/list be part of what you have on your list for the week. Pick out 3 or, at most, 5 of those items on the weekly list and get it done, keeping in mind the master list.

Goodnight List

It is advisable to write down what you want to do the next day a night before. This is because, once an idea is written down, your mind gets to work in a bid to help you achieve it. This is called the goodnight list. No matter how tired you are from the day's work, ensure you set out a few minutes to get this done, as it would largely determine how enthusiastic you'd be about the next day's list.

The ABCD Method

Now, before I round up this chapter, try to go through each list using the ABCD method. That is, you make each list according to their order of priority:

A = Tasks that ensure my survival

B = Tasks helps me better myself and my personality

C = Tasks that are important, and beneficial to other people

D = Tasks that are beneficial, but not urgent: they can be delegated

E = anything that does not fit in ABCD can therefore be forgotten

Planning is bringing the future into the present

so you can do something about it now.

Alan Lakei

15   Plan your perfect Week

So now you need a blueprint. Because you already know, what has to be done and how it can to be done. In order to get started, I came across a very interesting method from the military: plan your perfect week. A perfect week does not exist you may say – every day is different – also that might be. However, what if you had no other choice than having a choice? You define your week and you manage the time you can effectively manage. To begin to effectively manage your time often begins with a change in perspective regarding time. Be aware: The resource time is non-renewable. Each moment or hour that is used up is a percentage of a resource, which will not be replenished. When there is a shortage of any resource it becomes important to closely monitor its uses. Consider the response to a shortage of water. Certain activities are eliminated from use, such as watering plants, whenever there is a state of draught. When time is viewed as a non-renewable resource it often becomes easier to understand the importance of managing it wisely. Specially as an entrepreneur, mompreneur, consultant or artist, it's either you plan your workweek or you let activities dictate what you do. Of course, there are times where an emergency project pops up to try to overshadow or interrupt already planned projects, but that should never be an excuse to not always plan your week. And even if you cannot live up daily to its maximum, you still have an outline to give some orientation to yourself.

Here is my perfect week as an example

	Mon	Tue	Wed	Thur	Fri	Sat
5:00	Yoga	Yoga	Yoga	Yoga	Yoga	Yoga
7:00	E-Mails	E-Mails	E-Mails	E-Mails	E-Mails	E-Mails
9:00	*Meeting Int*	Focus B	Focus C	Phone Calls	*Meetings Ext*	Sport
11:00	*Meeting Int*	Focus B	Focus C	Phone Calls	*Meetings Ext*	Sport
13:00	E-Mails	E-Mails	E-Mails	E-Mails	E-Mails	Writing
15:00	Focus A	Phone Calls	Focus D	*Meetings Ext*	*Meetings Ext*	Writing
17:00	Focus A	Phone Calls	Focus D	*Meetings Ext*	*Meetings Ext*	Writing
19:00	Gym	Swimming	Gym	Squash	Gym	Friends
21:00	Read	Read	Read	Read	Read	Friends

As you see, I blocked daily time to do emails twice as well as to do sport and read. Furthermore you may notice, there is time to do phone calls to prospects and most importantly: time for meetings externally. Yes you have seen right: I only do outside company meetings on particular weekdays. That way, I can bundle all travel and distractions in between and reduce the issues come along with it to a minimal effect on two days.

NOTE: Always ensure you have an extra time every day for emergency projects. Yes, sometimes we can't help it, but creating a miscellaneous time would get you prepared ahead of time so as to prevent them from affecting what you have doing. The idea is to be ready for the worse. Sometimes, it could take more time, but knowing that you always have provision for it eases your mind and puts Parkinson's Law in motion for you.

"You cannot teach a man anything, you can only help him find it within himself"

Galileo Galilei

16   Energy hogs and Disturbance

Energy hogs are habits that steal our time and energy away and in turn reduc
our productivity. Part of which includes procrastination. Like I said earlier,
procrastination is not particular to a certain set of individuals; most of us
procrastinate every day. The key to controlling this destructive habit howeve
to understand when you begin to procrastinate, figure out why it's happenin
and then take active steps in ensuring you beat it.

Make Sure You Enjoy Your Work

Naturally, we try to run away from tasks that we really don't enjoy. Try as we
may to remain on any task we do not enjoy, we end up getting unnecessarily
drained and exhausted. This is one of the major causes of procrastination. It
very difficult to effectively do work we do not enjoy, talk more of getting it d
within a certain timeframe. For instance, you have a forte for motivational
speeches and now you are given an educational speech to write/deliver, how
you think that'd be? You guessed right.

What happens next is that, you instinctively try to shy away from that proje
the form procrastination. That resonates with so many of us, right? Yes. The
solution is to enjoy what you do. If you are not comfortable with that partic
task, delegate it to someone else who can do it perfectly. This will save you
of time to focus on what you know how to do best and enjoy.

Choose the Right Environment

Your workspace is very important when it comes to maintaining your energy level at work. A clogged workspace drains energy out of you and affects your focus. So ensure your space is clean and tidy enough to help you focus and get rid of any distraction around. If you can't achieve this at the office, you can create such environment at a secluded location or your home. You know, it's not all the time you feel like working from the office. If that resonates with you, make sure you choose a more secluded environment void of too many distractions for work. You could try a home office. That may not work for everybody as it makes some feel lazy, but if it does work for you, it's a great place to work from. It makes you feel right at home and relaxed while doing what you know how to do best. And of course, it makes you more productive.

Be Realistic with Your Expectations

Unrealistic expectation puts too much pressure on you, zaps the energy out of you and reduces your productivity drastically. You need to practice until you know how to set realistic timeframes for each task or related ones. When you are halfway into the task and the time is already whining down, it discourages you and lets you either postpone it or get frustrated and leave it entirely. Realistic time allocation on the other hand helps you stay on course.

Take a Break at Intervals

You are not a robot, so endeavor to rest your brain after each major task instead of rushing up to the next task on the list. By doing so, you conserve the energy you have left so you can use it for the next task. You can take a short walk within your office, throw a basketball or swing a golf club, if you have any of those in your office. If not, just leave your desk and walk around the office then come back to face the next task. That way, your head is a little bit detached from what you just finished, relaxed and ready for the next task on the agenda.

"You can never make the same mistake twice because the second time you make it, it's not a mistake, it's a choice."

Steven Denn

17   Your Report of Success

It's one thing to just focus on the job at hand, forgetting every other success you've had, and it's another thing to celebrate how far you've come while planning for the next big success. I think I'd prefer the later. As an entrepreneur, it's very easy to forget what you have already accomplished because, obviously, there are 1001 things that still need to be done. The thing however is, focusing only on the tasks without counting your blessings does more harm in the long run than good. It would feel like you are depriving yourself of the fulfillment and luxury your hard work could afford you.

The following ways will help you better report your success and treat yourself to some fulfilling payback from all those hard work.

Keep a journal

When you keep a good record of your successes, you are more likely to know when it calls for celebration. For instance, as soon as the balance check clears from that multimillion-dollar contract, you document it as another milestone. Make it a habit to document each accomplishment so you can go through them as often as possible to remind you of how far you've come.

Make successes visible

Yes! Don't be a miser; life is too short to make all the money in the world only to leave them at the bank. I'm not saying you should start spending all the money you make; however, it is never a bad idea to spoil yourself, family and friends to some exotic party or holiday once a while. Of course, isn't this what add spices to life? Life is all about the wonderful memories you can create with your family and friends, and you can't do this when all you are concerned about is piling up that money in the bank. No matter how little, let your success be visible, at least, for your family.

Use positive affirmations

Words are powerful. They determine how far you can go in life. They also determine whether you'd be a failure or a success at anything you do. No matter how promising a project is, once you make negative affirmations about it, chances are it's going to screw up one way or the other. But when you make positive affirmations, the law of attraction works in your favor to make it easier and achievable.

Feel proud about yourself

If you don't, who will? Every so often, give yourself a pat in the back and nod to some accomplishments. It is not pride; it is you being proud of what you've been able to accomplish. It is you rewarding yourself for the hard work and the sleepless nights that have got this far. Don't wait till someone calls to tell you they are proud of you look in the mirror and tell that to yourself every day.

So try as much as you can to keep a record of your success. As they age old saying, _all work and no joy makes Jack a dull boy,_ I rephrase it to mean _all work and no celebration makes life boring._

"In order to do great things,

we should live as though we were never to die"

Luc de Clapiers

18   10 Things you do not have to do anymore

As an entrepreneur, there are certain things you should outgrow with time. These activities if not delegated would waste your precious time and get you quickly exhausted instead of focusing on the most important things. Some of these things include:

Office supplies

Instead of going out yourself to get consumables like whiteboard markers, copy papers, etc. you can simply delegate or place an order on *Amazon* and they'd all be delivered to your office. It would be much easier for you to actually ask one of your staff to take care of stuff like this in the long run so you never have to even notice they're already running out.

Accounting

Making accounts itself takes quite some time, and even when you're done, you never know if you are right or wrong thereby getting unnecessarily worn out in the process. Truth is, not everyone is competent in this field so it's normal. What to do however is to hire an accountant to take care of all your accounting needs so you can focus on what you know how to do best – your business.

Research

We all know how much time it takes to do a good research. To save you that time, you can rely on professionals on sites like Fiverr.com to take care of those tedious research works and buy you enough time to focus on more important things.

Writing text and illustrations

Writing doesn't come naturally to everyone, and if you are one of such, the best thing to do is to outsource. Need a text on a specific topic but have no desire, time or inspiration to research it yourself? Then get a competent writer to do all those hard work for you. There are plenty of professional writers online that can do a create job at giving you just what you need or even extend your expectations. Be it a presentation, speech, website copy, etc., you can always find someone to help you with it. All you have to do is to specify the keywords and topic you want, and then leave it to them. What about designing presentations and graphics for your business? You can easily outsource these things for graphic professionals on sites like freelancer.com, upwork.com, and fiverr.com. You will be amazed the kind of result you get using those help.

Virtual Assistant

Certain things can easily get you overwhelmed as an entrepreneur. For instance, emails, transcriptions, hotel and travel bookings, basic reports, slides presentation, business blog updates, etc. The work of a virtual assistant is to help you do all that and more. Besides saving you more time than you can think, it will help you stay focused on the most important things. It also removes email distractions, since you already have someone taking care of that for you. Virtual assistants can help become more productive as an entrepreneur.

Bookings with yourself

If your business requires some bookings every so often, you cannot afford to be the one doing all those bookings. You can setup a bookings page on your site so potential clients can easily fill and then your virtual assistant will then compile them for you. This will make you focus on the main things and increase your productivity drastically.

Cleaning

Who has all the time to be vacuuming the office floor or dusting the desks? Not me. Not you. But there are people who are actually very good at these things. Hire such and save yourself some time and stress, too. Technology has even afforded us a vacuum cleaner robot that can help you do all the cleaning in your absence. Isn't that amazing? Take advantage of them.

Dry Cleaner

What time would you allocate to doing the laundry when your calendar is full and work piles up everywhere? This is where laundry and ironing services comes to play. You can sign up for either home or office deliveries within a few days. This makes life really easy for the entrepreneur who always likes to dress in style.

Groceries

If you are the type that lives on pizza and sushi, you may often experience the stress of joining the queue just to order these things. Why not just place an order or ask your virtual assistant to place the order and get it delivered to your office/home? Trust me, there's no feeling like getting your favorite groceries delivered to your doorstep.

As much as time management is an interesting concept, it doesn't make it less an easy thing to master. It takes time and constant practice to get used to some of these things. It's okay to fail at most of them when you start, but just like everything else once doing, commit to it and with time, you will become a master at it. Good luck and never forget: Just do it, now, one thing and things will get coming.

19   Summary

Dear reader, thank you for getting so far. I hope by now you have seen some of the things that'd keep your creative juices flowing and remain productive. As entrepreneurs, there are many projects calling your attention from right, left and center. Your job is not to juggle into all of them and come out exhausted all the time; your job is to filter these projects and see the ones that are more important to your company and progress per time, then focus on that important task and get it done.

Only after you are done with one should look into getting started with the next one. Juggling between different tasks does not only make you deliver less than your usual standard, it will also affect your credibility as a business in the long run. Do what you have to do when you have to do them. Remember Parkinson's Law? Set realistic timeframes for each task and ensure you get it done without any form of procrastination.

Keep accurate to-do list of what you want to do within each month per project. Set out a monthly list, and then split it into weekly lists and daily lists. This will keep you in check and help you measure your progress moving forward. Lists are particularly important if you have set a specific yearly or monthly target for your company. Each accomplished goal is a huge step towards the accomplishment of the grand vision of the company. As they said, the journey of a thousand miles starts with a single step. Those baby steps or baby accomplishments daily, weekly or monthly is what would eventually lead to the fulfillment of the bigger goal for the company.

Every so often, set time aside to enjoy your successes. Of course, why do you work so hard when you cannot enjoy the fruits of your labor? Doing otherwise makes life uninteresting and boring. Take a few days exclusive trip to somewhere special with a loved one or entire family, as the case may be. Show them why you spend so much time away from them; to give them the lifestyle they deserve.

All tips as checklists summarized

Live the good life and enjoy every bit of it because the truth is, you deserve it! To make it even easier, here are all tips summarized for you – any excuse to start right now? I don't think so.

Core Time Management Checklist

1. Write down what you will do for the day as soon as you wake up or preferably a night before.

2. Always remember the Pareto's Principle (The "80/20 Rule"). Write down and work on 20% of activities that produce the 80% of your results, instead writing a long list.

3. Delegate some of your tasks, especially those you know you struggle with. Give it to those you feel can do it best.

4. Always keep a pad handy for notes and ideas while working.

5. Only focus on the most important things, do every other thing at your leisure.

6. Learn to think at your feet and make decisions as fast as possible. Some things demand urgent action. If confused, follow your gut.

7. Become a good team player. Teamwork can help you get a lot done in a very short time.

8. Stop at intervals to evaluate your time and measure it up with the time left to work for the day.

9. Don't forget Parkinson's Law – your tasks expand to fill the time you assign to them. Master timing.

Action Tips for Time Management

1. Stay conscious and fight procrastination. Give yourself a reward system and stick with it.

2. Just get to it and get it done. You don't win an award from being a perfectionist.

3. Get to know your most active moments within the day and do your best job at that time.

4. Even if you don't feel like doing it, just start and you will see that it will flow afterwards – just start.

5. Start with something less stressful and bogus; little successes lead to bigger successes as your day progresses.

6. Do what you have to do now – take that action right now.

7. Know what it is you want to achieve for the day – that major thing – and make sure you pursue it.

8. If you are scared of a particular task, you can try doing it first so you can get it out of the way.

Email / Social Media Tips for Time Management

1. Dedicate a particular time of the day for doing emails and focus on doing that alone – nothing else but emails.

2. Register an account on buffer and add all your social media accounts so you can be able to monitor them from one place and save you time.

3. Turn off all your email and social media notifications while working on other things. A few of the aforementioned apps can help here.

Energy Tips for Time Management

1. If a particular activity is being so difficult, outsource or delegate it to a competent staff that can do it for you. It's okay if you can't do everything by yourself.

2. Schedule a periodic break while working so you can relax your head for a few minutes by taking deep breaths at intervals, doing some stretching or taking a quick work around the office.

3. Focus only on your strengths and never consider yourself as less productive when it comes to your weaknesses.

4. Exercise, sleep and eat regularly and at the right time. This will sustain your energy level.

5. Do your best work at that time you feel at your best.

Focus Tips for Time Management

1. Forget multitasking if you want to give it your best. Don't compromise this by yielding to the many distractions around you.

2. Let your mindset be that of one who uses time to create value and not one who just spends or wastes time as the case may be.

3. Let your mind be set on the end result and not the process. The process will let you feel overwhelmed and easily stressed out.

4. Be determined to stay true to the task at hand by learning to deal with distractions. Some of the apps/software can help in this regard.

5. Do not tempt yourself. Keep your distractions far away. For instance, your phone can be kept in one of your drawers while working.

6. Make sure you complete one tasks and enjoy that feeling of accomplishment before moving to the next.

7. If you feel blocked, change environment – anywhere serene and distraction-free, of course.

Meeting Tips for Time Management

1. Cut down your meeting times and train your staff to keep board meetings strict and straight to the point.

2. Let your meeting time be known to everyone in attendance. For instance, by 2 p.m. for 30 minutes.

3. Make sure you surround yourself with the right people at the meeting, especially when it is an outside meeting.

4. On rare occasions, meet outside your office, so you can easily walk out.

Motivation Tips for Time Management

1. Focus on your WHY. Be it for a regular first class vacation or a penthouse in the Bahamas, anything that inspires you to work the way you do.

2. Place pictures or elements from your WHY around your working space so you can easily look at them for a quick reminder. It could be your family, etc.

3. Picture the feeling of a job well done before starting that seeming draining task.

4. Be careful with your language. Don't say negative things about yourself or the task at hand as it will shut down your subconscious mind and your ability to get it done.

You are now at the end of this book, and thus also the end of my collected wisdom. I hope you were able to learn one or two things that can help you become more productive as an entrepreneur. In this sense, and in the words of Johann Wolfgang von Goethe, I want you to repeat these words up to 10 times (say it out loud, too):

"There is nothing good in the world, unless you do it."

20   About the author

Roger Basler holds a university degree in international management and is a business architect. As a digital native with a fondness for languages and foreign countries, he worked abroad as a consultant for many years. In his role as business architect, he accompanies established companies and start-ups in the areas of business development, digital marketing and ecommerce, thereby connecting innovative service providers and strategies both nationally and internationally.

He is a frequent speaker at seminars and events, as well as teaching at the Somexcloud Switzerland, the Institute for Startups Switzerland and many more schools across Europe. He is an author in the field of economics, productivity, sales management, startups and ecommerce as well as social media and digital marketing.

You can follow him on Twitter @rogerbasler

21   Book Tip

The One Thing explains the success habit to overcome the six lies that block our success, beat the seven thieves that steal time, and leverage the laws of purpose, priority, and productivity.

Here are some key insights

- Extraordinary results are determined by how narrow you can make your focus
- Do fewer things for more effect instead of doing more things with side effects
- Success is built sequentially
- Not everything deserves equal time
- Achievers always work from a clear sense of priority
- Multitasking is a lie and it does not work
- Discipline and habit intersect
- It takes 66 days to create a habit
- Become a person of powerful habits

Get the book on Amazon: The One Thing

22   Disclaimer

1st edition 2016 - Author, editor, editing, setting, design (incl. Cover design), texts, and images, Cover Picture: Roger Basler

Made in the USA
Middletown, DE
30 December 2018